W9-CRY-502

the bones
of
this land

for Mar & Car
with love &
appreciation —

Kat

Copyright © 2017 Swimming with Elephants Publications

All rights reserved. No portion of this publication may be reproduced, stored in a retrieval system, or transmitted in any form or by any other means, electronic, mechanical, photocopying, or recording without prior permission of Kat Heatherington unless such copying is expressly permitted by federal copyright law. Address inquiries in permissions to: Swimming with Elephants Publications.
swimmingwithelephants.com

Cover Art Copyright © 2017 Gwendolyn Prior

ISBN-13: 978-0998462363 (Swimming with Elephants Publications)

ISBN-10: 0998462365

the bones
of
this land

poems by
kat heatherington

for Frank W Heatherington
1941-2015

what is remembered, lives.

CONTENTS

I

everyone's father dies of something

II

desert solitaire

I.

everyone's father dies of
something

bending to the shape of water

how must it be
to live in a place marked only
by a slow rate of decay,
buildings sinking wall by wall
into earth that sinks
beneath even your lightened step.
even the sunlight
doesn't stay put, but slides
into banks of rising clouds
and the small dense fog
that rises from this creek
that never goes dry,
not even in summer,
not for a minute.
this land, this house
and now your body
all bend to the shape
of that water.

this aching echo

you were fifteen when the doctors
cracked your father open like a broken heart,
declared him inoperable,
gave him six months, and stopped caring.
you have never in your life trusted doctors.
now you are in their hands, reliant
on their knowledge, their caring.
Robert did not die in six months. he hurt
till you were seventeen,
and died in a hospital bed.
you saw the bleak relief
in your mother's cool brown eyes.
she blamed the cancer on the war.
all those years of fumes
she used to seal the house against.
"the silver cord is loosed,"
she said, and so were you,
out of school and into the army,
wild with grief and anger,
urgently needing to become someone new.
you lost the anger long ago, but
you've been trying to die for decades.
now that it is here, you fight it.
the wound in your father's chest gapes before you.
his broken lungs labor inside your ribs.
you know that it will kill you,
and already it hurts unimaginably,
this unsurprising echo of your father's pain,
the aching cycles of your choices.

but you cannot choose
to loose the silver cord.
not yet.

remember

remember not that you argued
with your sister, but that you sang
in the kitchen alone,
and the house remembered
a sound it had not heard in years.
remember fireflies blinking
slowly in the roadside dark
and a night sky as open
as the Arizona night sky —
remember, on the last night, every star
in the heavens shone on that place.
a comet streaked to the east
bright as a firecracker, potent, silent.
remember the vine that entered the door
and the softness of your father's voice
and the way his eyes lit up
every time he looked up and saw you there.
remember his pleasure, and his pride.
the way the creek sank when the rain stopped,
the six-part insect harmony every night,
and his hand on your shoulder,
blessing you. remember
his hands when he talks,
his big, precise gestures,
his carefully kept and yellowing fingernails.
the black trees in silhouette

against a star-strewn horizon.
his voice, retelling
the story of your birth – *when the nurse*
handed you to me, i felt a love
i had never known before.
and it has never stopped.
the scent of honeysuckle,
a redolent night,
that infinite sky.
it has never stopped.

reading together

one summer and then another, growing up,
i sat reading with you by the lake
laying on my belly with a book beneath my eyes.
you sat, legs stretched before you, your back
propped by a small red and white cooler,
your shirt thrown over it to soften the edge,
a book upright in your lap.
the sun marked its passage in conifer shadow
advancing down the shore.
glints of light flickered endlessly on the water.
the sun warmed our bodies, and you
compared us to lizards enjoying a hot rock,
through the long afternoons.
your eyes would light up when you looked at me.
we talked easily, inconsequentially, in the space between.
we had all the time in the world.
i'd get up to hike the shoreline,
and you'd pat my shoulder and
smile and say, all right honey.

now at the end, again we sit and read together.
you can barely talk. you have trouble
understanding me. the oxygen machine
pumps and hums, doing half your breathing for you.
we have already said everything that can be said.
yellow light pools on the scarred yellow table.
i give you my hand, all i can offer,
and sit beside you while you read.

unless you mean to fire

sharp small crack of the rifle
in a cold afternoon, the gun
strong and warm in my hands,
almost alive.
inhale, center, focus on the sights
not the target. fire on the exhale.
you can't see the bullet
just a puff of dust and maybe
a hole in the paper
as the barrel jumps
in your hand and the stock
kicks your shoulder.
twenty years since i've done this
but i still know how.
my daddy's hands holding mine
in the right position, finger straight
alongside the barrel, *don't touch the trigger*
until you mean to fire. his crooked
brown hands in the sunlight, releasing mine.
now you do it. the rocky hillside
bright with sound and sun.
soda cans full of buckshot in the dirt.
it is all about alignment.
i rest on one knee, bone-stacked.
barrel to wrist to elbow
to knee to ankle to earth.
stock to shoulder to hip

to ankle to earth. exhale again
and the gun's kick
slides right through me.

dying of something

it's the ordinary tedium of it that gets to me.
the butterfly bush is blooming in violet spikes,
and my father is dying of lung cancer.
the summer rains arrive, my boss
goes on vacation, there's work to do
and errands to run and
my father is dying of cancer.
the world is ending; life goes on.
everyone's father
dies of something.

taking flight

yesterday i saw a small hawk
on the walnut tree beside the spring house,
today, a squirrel.
all day the sun lies bright and thin
on still-green grass and barren branches.
only the squirrel and i see it,
and the little birds flitting at the feeder.
the house is a container of waiting.
the house is preparing to become a shroud.
the house is shadows and silence, punctuated
by pools of yellow light, and soft voices.
it is already moving into the past.
the small hawk swooped down the creek
and was gone. a thin wind
shifted the honeysuckle
that grows on the spring house.
after one more departure,
i, too, will take flight.

the last night

the heater, the clock,
the oxygen pump
and your breath —
these sounds
mark minutes, allow
this night to pass —

everything circles back
to that mountain
the sun
the silence

like the light

i am almost twilight
i am almost home
i am cracked by a thousand birds
crossing the darkening sky.
you are a silhouette
you are a storm cloud
you are half of every strand
of DNA in my body.
the storm strains inside my skin.
the storm is breaking.
you will never be
merely memory.
you are a kind hand resting
on my shoulder.
you are a wild anger
against the world's injustice.
you are survived by
two daughters, two brothers,
one sister, and the work
of your hands.
your memory moves
in this cracking twilight.
like the light,
you have gone home.

since you died

since you died, i have been
surrounded by flowers.
since you died, i have been
embraced by many hands.
since you died
i have been under water
but not enough of it—
i have been learning
for a third time
how to breathe.
i am a seed caught up in frost.
i am too cold, too warm,
struggling to turn
waiting for the crack, the shatter
that will let my first new leaf
emerge, wet and tender
into the sun.
i am frightened of the crack
and hungry
for the blossom.

fragments on my father's death

how do you divide a man
when you could never divide a heart?
yet i divide what is left of your body,
plant you in pieces,
scatter you to the wind.
you shall have the whole mountain west.
you cannot be reduced to a body.
to handfuls of ash. you will grow
in the shade of these cottonwoods,
in a place you never lived,
surrounded by birdsong.
you will bloom.
and i will never again
be far from you.

what is this,
that the dust of a man
can run between my fingers
and grow roses?

so much of you lifts
in the wind, disperses.
i breathe you in,
ash into living flesh,
earth to earth.
i am already your flesh.
i will learn again
how to bloom.

a place my father loved, but never lived

you bore my father in your arms as he lay dying.
you bore his ashes up the mountain on your back.
what remains of his body
dissolved in the wind of a place
the earth has taken back so hard
it hollows out my heart.
now you carry down the mountain on your back
the stone that shaped the history of this land.
you carry its story back into ours,
and plant it, veined pyrite gleaming in the sun,
in a place my father loved, but never lived.

reading maps

my dad, and the girl scouts, taught me how to read a map.
to interpret topography, climb a mountain, return home.
to carry a compass at all times, and to use it.
if you have this, you can never get lost.
for years i kept one in my purse.
now i remember your crooked brown finger,
tracing the line, then pointing out the ridge.
now i map my past, trace roads and ridges
on satellite maps, hunt out your old campsites,
feel the curve of the land and the road in
the shape of my childhood,
to find my way back to you.
to bring what is left of your body
and what is left of my childhood,
back to one place,
and feel that long sunlight,
and the ash in my hands.

the bones of this land

i grew up on a mining claim
in the mountains of central arizona.
bear with me.
i grew up in a nice-enough house
on the poor side of a small town
in the mountains of central arizona.
i walked to school every day,
got a job in a thrift store when i turned 15,
and spent every second weekend
and then some
up at the mine with my dad.

this was not a hobby.
my dad drank hard.
the desert dried him out,
more or less. saved his life.
like a cactus, he retained
what he most valued.
books, beer, his daughters.
the desert gave back clarity,
integrity. silence.
his skin baked brown under that long sun.

the old copper mine had played out
decades ago, the top collapsed
into an open pit. an ore mill straddled
the hillside above. junk abounded.

old cars, oil barrels, you name it.
the product and refuse of industry.
dad's buddy Chris would come
up to the claim with beer money
and they stood there talking
in the shade of one real big oak,
where dad kept his camper parked
near the edge of the bluff,
how they were gonna get that mill running,
and make a million bucks.
or even a living.
they didn't try very hard.
it was enough
to stand in that shade, that sun,
and take in each day. the sun
and the solitude filled him up.
i spent my nights by the light of a kerosene heater,
in the old stone cabin, its shelves
piled with antique chemistry in jars,
enticing and dangerous.
my sister collected interesting rocks,
set them up in a pile by the old mine tailings.
we read books, talked with dad,
sat in the shade, or explored scrub-covered hillsides,
and the seep down the hill,
at the old cave-mine entrance,
where a cottonwood grew, and watercress,
while dad sipped his beer, read, smoked cigarettes,
year after year. we ate lentils cooked with an onion,

circus animal cookies, orange crush. it sounds
like poverty, and it was, but those were good years.

twenty years after leaving that place, my sister and i
went back to scatter his ashes. it was not
the place he died, or the place he'd lived the longest.
but it was the only place that made sense.
we had the idea that we'd stand
on the edge of that bluff, under the old oak
that sheltered those years, and throw ash to the wind.

we found the mine. the road was gone,
locked and rucked into hillocks and destroyed.
so we walked up.
the old mill was gone. how do you erase
something the size of an ore mill?
a wide flat spot remained, buzzing with
bees drinking nectar from horehound and mallow.
not a single gear or barrel or oil stain was left.
i found one steel washer in the dirt,
and a piece of plastic –
a relief. this tiny human thing.
we walked on. the bluff
was gone. the old oak, vanished.

the land just – stopped.
a tree big enough to live under.
a hillside wide enough to grow up on.
washed down the gully. we felt
that we had imagined our childhoods.

the bones of the land
spoke to my bones.
the horizon remained,
limitless, green, unspeaking.
pinned under the vast blue
of that desert sky, and, always,
offering up to it.
nothing had changed, except us.
everything had changed, except us.

we ate lunch surrounded by manzanita and silence.
i found one stone, a pebble,
flecked with mortar
from the vanished cabin beneath the oaks.
i took it home.
now, even that trace is gone.

we scattered his ashes off the new edge of the bluff.
scrub oak and manzanita accepted
the dust of our father's body,
as they had accepted the dust of his life.

i piled the last handful of ash
beside a tiny purple wildflower.
as we watched, an ant walked on it,
took a fleck of bone carefully in its mandibles,
and walked away.

now even that trace is gone.
it lives, like him,
only in our bones.

perseids

the perseids fall.
the weather breaks,
sharp heat turning to sudden wind
and sometime rain.
i stand at the kitchen sink,
scrubbing what remains of your life.
a photo of the most beautiful work
your hands ever made.
the thing itself long since rotted
by mountain rains and sometime sun.
a license plate with your radio call sign,
the name you kept even after moving
to a place ham radio could not reach;
the plate you kept long after
you stopped driving.
eleven years of cigarette
smoke and winter gloom
scrubbed off the glass.
sent down the drain.
i cannot love only
the beautiful, only the proud, only
the moments of shining redemption.
i can only love you whole.
i wrap myself in the last coat
that comforted you in life,
curl up in the brief, welcome coolness

of a rainy desert night,
and miss,
without complexity,
your voice.

II.

desert solitaire

every time i fall

a small glass heart,
the oakland hills,
a candle burning in bright day.
music i can lean on.
women's voices, arms that catch me
every time i fall.
i am falling the way sunlight
enters a room through a warm closed window
and unfurls along the floor.
i fall and surface and fall again
like a leaf in a whirlpool.
i fall and fall.
your voice on the altar,
one white lily among the gold.
i fall until i am standing,
and it no longer hurts.

time is distance and distance is distance

1.

time is distance and distance is distance
and the heart aches to cross both,
yearning across boundaries,
loving across boundaries.
i build a nest in my heart,
furnish it lavishly, comfortably,
keep it warm for when you return.
you step inside, melting me with a smile
and a simple, frank, "i love you,"
and the miles and days melt away.

2.

time is distance and distance is distance,
and the heart aches to cross both.
what would i do to have you back again,
as we once were?
what history, what learning, would i erase
to stretch again in the warmth of your regard?
a push against the limitations of the possible, of the real.
i would not be other than i am.
though this appears to mean i have lost you.

3.

time is distance and distance is distance
and a heart aches, standing,
still, and growing.

an edge made for embracing

edges aren't arbitrary.
to pretend they do not matter
or should not be there, is to cross them
and cross them again, cutting
or being cut each time.
yet you softened your edges for me,
filed away the roughness
before you met me skin to skin.
an edge that cannot cut.
an edge made for embracing.
sleepy and sloe-eyed in the morning,
eyes gone dark and liquid with desire.
our rough hands soften on each other.
i am filled with gratitude
for the soft curve of your cheekbone
silvered by moonlight.

desert solitaire

one day i watch you reading *Desert Solitaire* in bed.
you are not yet leaving me.
your voice is rich and tender
and we are laughing. i read to you
an essay about the beauty of the desert,
the necessary beauty of rough edges.
as i read i lean in
to your comfortable body, and then
we are silent. we lay inside the words,
the night, the desert, our love. i feel
that we will make it. i feel
we see one another clearly, and so
we can do anything.
two seasons later you are gone,
there is much we have not done and will never do,
and i am pulling tumbleweeds in the long slant
of evening light, leaning into the wind, stepping
careful in the mud of my irrigated desert field.
my hands are stronger than they have ever been,
and gentle. i pull out every interloper by the roots.
mound them, with attention, along the path's edge,
for mulch. something valuable lies
inside of everything. even this.

when you speak

mars is in retrograde.
the bonfires lit in my spine last summer are dull,
dark orange coals scabbing over with black and ash.
smoke idles up inside my back, sighs toward the skin,
escapes with every exhaled breath,
as each word moves closer to silence.
i look the same as i did eight years ago,
last time i walked the streets alone at night
and marked the passage of mars.
your hair is noticeably shorter,
your eyes hard with new wariness,
your heart no longer opening toward mine.
when you speak, i have no defenses.
when you speak, you strike the spark,
but fail to reach your hands out toward the blaze.

after abortion

i thought my dreams would be haunted
by the dark-haired elfin child
i did not bear.
instead i dream of my grandmother,
five years dead,
holding me in her arms
as she never did in life,
as she seldom held
any of her children.
what heritage of struggle and loss,
of absence,
we carry with us
and bear through generations.

present with something burning

you rest in a body of water
with fire cupped in your hand.
you are a waterfall, grief & change & love,
and you are present with something burning.
even at rest, your body moves.
you are alive to your own changes,
casually shedding sparks in the chill night air.
when i rise from the water,
the night is a cavern and you are turning,
you are gone, you are telling me
you love me you are telling me
you'll see me soon. i am a waterfall
shedding sparks, and your cupped fire
turns to taillights in the rising night.

fulcrum

i put my heart in the rushing river
and stretch, and stretch again.
washing clear, inviting in,
expanding capacity, expanding trust.
i put my heart in the rushing river
and learn to love you
and myself, at the same time.
i put my heart in the rushing river
and i pour and pour and pour.
when i lift from the water
bright sun warms my skin.
a heron upstream cocks its head, listening.
the wind pauses, then plays.
light drips off the cottonwoods like water,
falls in the river, sparkles off downstream.
i breathe it in.
i am lifted. i am living. i am alive.

gardens that will outlive us

wind tears my eyes, clothes & hair.
weeds whip across the road.
i walk past other women's gardens
some blooming, some broken
relics of people long gone.

morning sun slants over the wall,
strikes sparks from the blooming shrubbery.
tall swaying fronds lean into the fire.
it's a penstemon -- not just any penstemon--
but a vivid magenta penstemon,
the tiny tongues of each blossom
lapping the sunlight.

this is how it is, then,
to plant gardens that will outlive us.
to stay in one place and watch them grow.
sun on any and every morning,
in balance with the wall's cool shadow.
green from every living thing
and blossoms in their time.
in the green, the blossom, the harvest:
fulfillment.

the limitation of the real

on a morning bruised
by the limitation of the real,
the kiss of sun
wakes my skin to gratitude.
if we did not reach our limits
we'd never learn how
to appreciate all
that we have and are.

acknowledgements

I would like to thank the following publications for providing first homes to some of these poems:

The 2006 Harwood Anthology, "when you speak."

The 2012 Harwood Anthology, *How To: Multiple Perspectives on Creating a Garden, a Life, Relationships and Community.* "gardens that will outlive us."

Malpaís Review 2015 and 2016, "after abortion" and "when you speak." "After abortion" was titled "after miscarriage" at that time; I have since decided that the truth matters to this piece, and have amended the title accordingly.

gratitude

This book would not have been possible without the support and encouragement of more people than I can possibly name in one page. Love and gratitude to Lisa Gill and Erin Daughtrey, who have read, encouraged, and offered amazingly helpful feedback on my work for many years, and who gave me the advice that let this manuscript become what it is.

Enormous love and gratitude to my life-partner Alan Post, my Sunflower River farm-family, Jenny Rice, Tristan Fin, and Rev Tsolwizar, and my love Terra Phoenix, all of whom held me safe and made sure that I knew I was loved while I lived these poems, and every day since.

Love, gratitude & appreciation to my Heatherington family, John, Pam, Geo, Ciska, Helen & Eric, for their love, support, and welcoming acceptance of me into this family when I, as a young adult, finally met them all -- and through all the years since. I am grateful for their support, and their acceptance of the poems about my father. Love and gratitude to Madelon Ezell Heatherington and Drusilla Ezell for their love, kindness, and the home they created with my dad. Enormous love and appreciation also to my mother, Debra Cording. And to everyone who has, knowingly or not, inspired a poem in this book, my thanks.

And of course, though he is not here to read it, I offer my love, appreciation, respect and gratitude to my father, Frank W Heatherington, without whom I would not be the person I am today.

about the author

Kat Heatherington is a
queer ecofeminist poet,
sometime artist, pagan,
and organic gardener.
She has been living in
Albuquerque since
1998, when she moved
here to earn a Master's
in English at UNM.

In 2007 she collaborated with a group of three other
unrelated adults to buy land in the Rio Grande Valley and
form Sunflower River intentional community,
sunflowerriver.org. Ten years and many life lessons later,
Sunflower River is still going strong, and still providing
plenty of material to write poems about.

Kat's work primarily addresses the interstices of human
relationships and the natural world. She has several self-
published chapbooks, available from the author at
yarrow@sunflowerriver.org. Her work can be read at
https://sometimesaparticle.org.

Also available from
Swimming with Elephants Publications, LLC

My Blood is Beautiful
Mercedez Holtry

the fall of a sparrow
Katrina K Guarascio

22
Gigi Bella

Periscope Heart
Kai Coggin

They Are All Me
Christina Dominque

Observable Acts
Kevin Barger

Morena
Eva Marisol Crespin

Verbrennen
Matthew Brown

Language of Crossing
Liza Wolff-Francis

Find More Publications at:
swimmingwithelephants.com